Havre de Grace
Photo Album

Leon Nicholas Kalas

4880 Lower Valley Road, Atglen, Pennsylvania 19310

Published by Schiffer Publishing Ltd.
4880 Lower Valley Road
Atglen, PA 19310
Phone: (610) 593-1777; Fax: (610) 593-2002
E-mail: Info@schifferbooks.com

For the largest selection of fine reference books on this and related subjects, please visit our web site at **www.schifferbooks.com**
We are always looking for people to write books on new and related subjects. If you have an idea for a book please contact us at the above address.

This book may be purchased from the publisher.
Include $3.95 for shipping.
Please try your bookstore first.
You may write for a free catalog.

In Europe, Schiffer books are distributed by
Bushwood Books
6 Marksbury Ave.
Kew Gardens
Surrey TW9 4JF England
Phone: 44 (0) 20 8392-8585; Fax: 44 (0) 20 8392-9876
E-mail: info@bushwoodbooks.co.uk
Website: www.bushwoodbooks.co.uk
Free postage in the U.K., Europe; air mail at cost.

Photography and text by Leon Nicholas Kalas.
Designed by Mark David Bowyer
Type set in New Baskerville BT / Korinna BT

ISBN: 978-0-7643-2863-3
Printed in China

Contents

Dedication

My mother and my two sisters Helen and Ioanna; my son, and my confidant friend, Julius Heard.

In memory of Vanroy Rowe: my best life-long friend without whom I would have never discovered Havre de Grace.

Acknowledgments

It is very difficult to express my gratitude and give thanks by name to anyone in particular who assisted me and motivated me in the publication of this book. I can only say that I am exceedingly grateful to all the wonderful people of Havre de Grace for their overwhelming enthusiastic response when they first heard that this project was under way — they gave me the energy I needed to see it through to its completion.

Special thanks are offered to my good friend Ronald G. Browning at the La Cle D'or Guesthouse, whose efficient, enthusiastic, and expert proofing of my manuscript, along with his friend Mark Ver Valin, were an indispensable resource. I will always be grateful to Ron for his superb hospitality in letting me use his guesthouse as my home away from home during my numerous long visits to town in search of buying my own property and establishing a residence and fine art gallery.

Special thanks are also offered to Doris Schultz, and Maryanne Yenoli for their technical assistance; and to my friends and residents of Havre de Grace, Carol Nemeth and Sharon Gallegher, for their encouragement in this project.

Introduction

It has often been said that people are drawn to live in Maryland's cities and towns because of their individual identities and the quality of life that exists in each of these communities. This is so true in particular of the City of Havre de Grace, a charming town by the Chesapeake Bay at its confluence with the Susquehanna River.

When tourists come to town, they are looking to find remnants of local history, experience the charm of preserved Victorian homes, attend festivals and events, and browse through wonderful antique shops. Most people visiting the town sense a community that has remained unchanged by the frenetic pace of the bigger cities around it and want to take advantage of the peaceful beauty of the Susquehanna State Park nearby.

This book is intended to help make people aware of the unique character of Havre de Grace, and provide an understanding of the natural beauty of the city, so people can return year after year to enjoy this vibrant and wonderful town.

Right:
Sunrise on the Chesapeake Bay. The Chesapeake Bay is the world's largest estuary.

Chapter One

Havre de Grace: A Brief History

In early times, before the discovery of America, the magnificently brown-skinned Susquehannocks roamed the area on which Havre de Grace now stands along the western shore of the beautiful Susquehanna.

Captain John Smith was the first European to sail to the upper part of the Chesapeake Bay and make a map of the contours of its shores. On Captain Smith's second voyage to the Bay — when he was accompanied by a small band of men from the Virginian Colony — one writer described the visit and their encounter with the Natives. It may be less than literary license that the meeting between the Englishmen and the Susquehannocks is described as taking place beneath a sunset almost mystical in brilliance that October afternoon of 1608. Certainly, the Susquehannocks' chief and his warriors watched and waited from the island at the mouth of the Susquehanna River before the peaceful pow-wow began. When the meeting broke up, the Indians returned to their quarters and Captain Smith and his men set up camp overnight on the island.

Captain Smith planted the seed for future settlement of this land when he wrote: "Heaven and earth seemed never to have agreed better to frame a place for man's commodious and delightful habitation." This seed bore fruit seventeen years later when in 1625 Edward Palmer, an eccentric Englishman, and a group of two hundred men settled on the island in the mouth of the Susquehanna. Palmer proposed to establish a university, as well as a fur and trapping business. The project was doomed. His associates made off with the funds and Palmer, himself, was too much of a dreamer to organize such an undertaking. The men began to drift away to Jamestown, Virginia, and some, perhaps, to the nearby shores of what would eventually become Havre De Grace.

This island, now crossed by the Route 40 Highway Bridge, has been known as Palmer's, Watson's, and Garrett Island. During an expedition, the contentious Captain William Claiborne took over Palmer's Island in 1637 and rebuilt the fort. For a year, he conducted a trapping and trading enterprise. Then, in 1638, Maryland Governor Leonard Calvert sent a force to claim the island for Lord Baltimore.

Undoubtedly, the settlement of Palmer's Island gave impetus to the gradual development of the area. Some of Claiborne's men surely came ashore to settle. Indian problems were almost nil, and Indian trails were transformed into a rather overland route, a little later to be connected between the eastern and western shores by a system of ferries. All of these elements encouraged growth. Lord Baltimore assigned some of the land to Godfrey Harmer on July 19, 1658 over a century before the town would become known as Havre de Grace. Early records refer to the settlement as Harmer's Town although a few months later, in 1659, Harmer assigned the property to Thomas Stockett.

A few families came to fish and trap. On May 13, 1661, a treaty was signed that ended individual quarrels between the Indians and the Englishmen in the area. This pact exhilarated growth—not only along the river but the island as well.

Five years later, in 1666, Post Road was opened; connecting South Philadelphia and New York, it ran through the settlement where Union Avenue now stretches north and south. Freelance ferries were operating from this point to other sites of the river.

About this time, George Alsop, an early chronicler of Maryland events and people, was living on Thomas Stockett's plantation. He came to this country as an indentured servant and in 1666 published a book in London about the state of Maryland.

On August 13, 1688, Jacob Looten of Cecil County received the site of Havre de Grace by deed from the Stockett family. Apparently, Looten, a Dutchman, had an exemplary character. He was caught at "nefarious dealing" with the Indians, an extremely unpopular course of action as far as more upright citizens were concerned. His widow married William York, who, with Jacob Young, was granted permission by the Maryland General Assembly in 1695 to establish a reliable ferry at Havre de Grace with inns at either side of the river as terminals. Legal toll rates were set up, and in October, the first legally established ferry across the Susquehanna at any spot from the Chesapeake Bay to the river's source was in operation.

In the 1700s, the names Harmer's Town and Stockett's were replaced with the designation the Susquehanna Lower Ferry to distinguish it from Bell's or the Upper-Ferry, south of Lapidum. The ferry owners, Young and York, used two large flat-bottomed scows joined together — a far cry from the dugouts, canoes, and rowboats employed without regard to dependability in former days. A sweep power was installed in one of the boats, using two blindfolded horses as the motive power for turning the paddle wheels. The passengers rode in the other scow. These horse-driven boats continued in use until replaced by a steamboat in 1840. On those ferries rode many of the men who literally formed this nation, chief of whom was George Washington.

Aerial view of Havre de Grace. The area was founded in 1782 and incorporated as a town in 1785. Located at the confluence of the Susquehanna River with the Chesapeake Bay in Harford County, Maryland, Havre de Grace became a city in 1882.

The local site again changed hands, in 1774, with its purchase by John Stocks, the High Sheriff of Baltimore County in which the land was then located. By that time, a number of individuals had acquired parcels of ground and built houses. By 1770 about two hundred people lived in town and most framed or fished.

With the organization of the colonial government in Maryland in 1773, Harford County was formed from part of Baltimore County. The following year the county government began functioning. Some thought was given about making the Susquehanna Lower Ferry the county seat, but geographical considerations gave that honor to Scott's Old Fields (Bell Air).

During the American Revolution, many of the Continental troops were moved across the Lower Ferry, the largest contingent being 6,000 French soldiers under the command of Count Rochambeau. They camped along Old Post Road in the area of the old racetrack and the present-day Maryland National Guard facility. In 1777, the British burned the little town.

The name Havre de Grace dates back to a time just after the American Revolution. The story of its naming may be apocryphal, but it is widely accepted and is surely appealing to the imagination. In 1782, General Lafayette traveled with General Washington from Mount Vernon to Philadelphia to attend the Continental Congress. The journey was made over Old Post Road and, for the first time, Lafayette crossed the Susquehanna at Lower Landing. The incomparable beauty of the river and its gently curving shoreline charmed him. He was told that another Frenchman, a fisherman recalling the French city of Le Havre, had exclaimed, "C'est Le Havre! Le Havre de Grace!" Lafayette wholeheartedly agreed with the fisherman's thought and the name was adopted.

By act of the General Assembly of Maryland in 1875, Havre de Grace was incorporated. It was to be organized with commissioners. Charles P. Hauducouer made maps of the town in 1779 and 1803. Although the town was fully established with five commissioners by 1880, official business was scarce and the commissioners only held two or three meetings a year. Attendance was never a hundred percent. Some sessions were held at Mrs. Sears' Tavern or at other public places. The town fathers devoted most of their energies to renting certain streets to the Market Space for fisheries. Inspectors of flour, lumber, fish, and salted provisions were also required.

The town commissioners managed several of Havre de Grace's lotteries. As early as 1795, the General Assembly authorized the town to set up lotteries to fund the opening of the navigation of the river and two public wharves. Nothing came of this until 1802 when the town received authority to use the proceeds of a lottery to build an Episcopal Chapel, a rectory, and a market house. The church was built in 1809. A school was later erected in 1821, but the market house was not built until around 1840. It stood in the center of Congress Avenue; its front, east of the line of Strawberry Lane between Washington and Market streets. The building housed a jail, a guardroom during the Civil War, a council chamber, and a schoolroom.

During the years 1786 to 1822, the town clerk or some other government official taught in the little school. Funds were appropriated in 1821 for the little schoolhouse, now at the corner of St. Clair Street (Pennington Avenue) and Union Avenue. The school operated under a system where tuition was paid, but some pupils were admitted for free. As attendance grew, classes were held at several other places in the town including private homes. In 1896, a brick school building with ten classrooms was built and four more rooms were added in 1906. As the school expanded, a new high school building was opened in January of 1925; today, it's still in use, with several additions having been made to it. The old brick building was razed for a gymnasium. Two elementary schools and a middle school were built elsewhere in town.

The plunder of the Chesapeake Bay region by the British in the War of 1812 wreaked havoc upon the town, but gave Havre de Grace a hero. During the bombardment of May 3, 1813, about three-fourths of the sixty or more houses were burned. Many of the four hundred residents were left homeless with only the clothes on their backs. John O'Neill, a prosperous merchant who owned a nail factory in town, was a second lieutenant in a company of Harford County militia belonging to the 42nd Regiment. With a few of the militiamen, he hastened to the Potato Battery when the British attack began. After a few shots were fired from the fifteen English barges, the men retreated except for O'Neill. His Irish ancestry, bred from the Hugh O'Neill line and nurtured with Irish-English antagonism, held him fast at the cannon. A little later, he wrote a letter describing the incident: "I loaded the gun myself without anyone to serve the vent, which, you know, is very dangerous, and fired her, when she recoiled and ran over my thigh." As O'Neill dragged himself towards the center of the town, he was captured by an English officer and taken aboard the *Maidstone*. Three days later, his fifteen-year old daughter, Matilda, accompanied by two adult friends, went aboard the ship to see him before he was executed. Admiral Sir George Cockburn was touched by Matilda's plea for her father's life and released the prisoner. When, in 1827, the Concord Point Lighthouse was built, John O'Neill was appointed its keeper. For nearly one hundred years, until the light was made automatic, a member of the O'Neill family was always keeper of the light.

Right:
Entering the town on Route 155 East, which is Exit 89 on Interstate 95. The stone viaduct over the roadway was built of Port Deposit granite by the Baltimore and Ohio Railroad as part of its bridging of the Susquehanna River here at Havre de Grace.

From the beginning, Havre de Grace was admirably located for water and land transportation. Stagecoaches operated regularly on Old Post Road. Then in 1863, the Baltimore and Port Deposit Railroad reached Havre de Grace. Its tacks were laid through St. Clair Street. The old White Chapel, formerly at the corner of Washington and St. Clair streets, was the passenger and freight station. For over twenty years, trains were ferried across the river from the foot of St. Clair Street. When the river froze so deeply in 1852 that a channel couldn't be kept open, the company laid ties and tracks in the ice and ran the trains over the ice for six months.

In 1838, the Philadelphia, Wilmington, and Baltimore Railroad of Pennsylvania, the Wilmington and Susquehanna Railroad of Delaware, and the Baltimore and Port Deposit Railroad of Maryland united. The new PWB Railroad Corporation was motivated to bridge the Susquehanna as (the B&O) Railroad neared completion. On November 28, 1866, the PWB Bridge of wooden spans went into service. In the 1870s, the wood was replaced with iron. The Pennsylvania Railroad System absorbed the Philadelphia, Wilmington and Baltimore Railroad in 1902, and in 1909, the present-day Pennsylvania Railroad Bridge was opened. The original bridge was converted to a highway structure. By 1928, it was made into the only double deck vehicular bridge in the country. It was closed in 1940 when the Highway Bridge over the lower end of Garrett Island was finished. In 1943, the metal was salvaged for use in World War II. At present, there are two highway bridges and two railroad bridges that cross the Susquehanna River at Havre de Grace.

For over a half a century, the Susquehanna and Tidewater Canal was a vital part of the busy scene in Havre de Grace. Built in 1839, the canal extended from commercial Wrightville, Pennsylvania to Havre de Grace, where there was a terminal for reshipment of merchandise such as coal, lumber and grain. Many local people were associated with the canal and its colorful history. The old Lock House has been restored by the Susquehanna Museum of Havre de Grace, Inc., and the locks and towpath can still be seen on the original property.

The commissioner form of government gave way to a mayor and city council when the Act of 1882 changed the Town of Havre de Grace to the City of Havre de Grace. Today, that political framework still functions with a mayor and six council members. The old Town Hall was originally constructed in 1870 as an opera house. It was partially burned in 1920 and rebuilt the following year. A new City Hall was completed in the 1990s.

The fishing industry, especially that of shad and herring, no longer plays the important role it once did in the city. Since World War I, much of the local economy has been based upon the employment of many residents at Aberdeen Proving Grounds, Edgewood Arsenal, and Perry Point Medical Center, and since World War II, at Bainbridge Naval Training Center, which is now deactivated. There has been a hospital in the city since 1912. The present-day Harford Memorial Hospital has been enlarged many times and is often filled to capacity; a large professional staff service the hospital. The local library, which replaced the Havre de Grace Library, was organized by a group of public-spirited citizens and is a branch of the county library system.

Havre de Grace is a city of churches with the major denominations and others well represented. Its banks with several drive-ins, building and loan associations, and credit unions form the backbone of a firm financial structure. The town has several museums: The Maritime Museum, The Decoy Museum, Concord Point Lighthouse & Light Keeper's House Museum, Susquehanna Museum of Havre de Grace at the Lock House, Skipjack Martha Lewis, and Steppingstone Museum. Havre de Grace has wonderful first-class restaurants, elegant Bed and Breakfast establishments, and two guesthouses. There are art galleries, antique shops, and a golf course at Bulle Rock, marinas, and a wonderful promenade along the Chesapeake offering panoramic views of the Bay.

Havre de Grace missed by one vote from being selected as the nation's capital city in 1789. How different her destiny would have been! But her elusive charm has held the hearts of sons and daughters and the names of many of them are forever a part of her history.

Chapter Two

The Homes of Havre de Grace

The Hill-Sheaffer House at 324 South Washington Street was built in 1865. At one time, the shop of local decoy carver, Bob McGraw, stood in back of the house.

The Carrer-Craig House at 453 Congress Avenue. The home, circa 1855, is a combination of Greek Revival and Italianate Style. The side porch was added in 1930.

451 Green Street. Circa 1899, this was once a duplex that was converted into a single-family home.

300 North Union Avenue. A stucco-over brick home, the style of the residence, and, particularly, the design of the hipped, slate roof with a steep curve rising to a peak reflect the French ancestry of the original owner, Baptise Aveilhe, who fled the revolution in Haiti to live in Havre de Grace.

The Bayou Hotel at 300 Commerce Street.
Opened in 1920 as a luxury hotel, it closed during the Great Depression.
It became a retirement home for the Franciscan Sisters in 1953, and in
1984 was converted into luxury condominiums.

The Vandiver Inn at 301 South Union Avenue.
This building is a fine example of a large Queen Anne cottage built in
1886 by Murray Vandiver, who served as Maryland's State Secretary and
treasurer as well as Mayor of Havre de Grace.

Terrace Gardens Apartments. Located on Route 40 at the Thomas J. Hatem Bridge (1939), the building once operated as a hotel for tourists.

Henry's House at 322 North Union Avenue.

The Susquehanna Fur Company on Route 40/ Pulaski Highway occupies the former relay station for C&P (Chesapeake and Potomac Telephone Company). Circa 1940.

Waters Edge Guest Cottage & Suites at 433 St. John Street. This tiny structure once served as the toll keeper's station for the vehicular double-decker bridge (1928-1940), which spanned the Susquehanna River.

At 501 St. John Street, the Abraham Jarrett Thomas House was built in 1834 as a residence for the local banker. Today it is the Joseph L. Davis Post American Legion Home.

Bank of Memories.
The First National Bank of Havre de Grace opened in 1883. This Port Deposit granite structure, at 319 St. John Street, was operated by Boddi Barrow for costume and estate jewelry and antiques until 2007.

Warren Street. The Pennsylvania Railroad tunnel is made of Port Deposit granite.

A view of one of the several marinas in Havre de Grace.

Condominiums along the Susquehanna River, which front at Seneca Point, offer spectacular views.

Right:
The old United States Post Office building at 308 North Union Avenue was restored in 2003 to be used as medical offices. Originally constructed in 1936 during the Great Depression as part of the Federal government work program, the brick and stucco structure sports a cupola reminiscent of George Washington's home, Mount Vernon.

The Old Ordinary, circa 1800s, has components dating back to 1809 and is located at 100 St. John Street. The lot was first leased in 1782 by Gabriel Peterson Vanhorn from the town's founder, Robert Young Stokes.

John O'Neill's House.
John O'Neill was the first keeper of the Concord Point Lighthouse and a hero of the War of 1812. It's now a museum.

This lovely Victorian residence at 200 North Union Avenue was built in the Grand Style in 1885 by local cannery businessman, Stephen J. Seneca. Mayor of Havre de Grace from 1893-94, Seneca employed noted Philadelphia architect William Plack to design this twenty-two-room mansion. Notice the copper-covered turrets, the design of the brick chimneys, bay windows, the porches, and dormer windows.

La Cle D'or Guesthouse (bed & breakfast) at 226 North Union Avenue. It was built in 1868 by Henry Harrison Hopkins, a pharmacist and son of Dr. Thomas C. Hopkins. The design of this house is an example of the eclectic, even eccentric, style that became popular after the Civil War.

Interior of the Spencer-Silver Mansion, circa 1896, that was constructed for John Spencer, a merchant and foundry owner. Later, the house was purchased by Charles Silver, owner of a local cannery. Today it is a bed & breakfast inn.

Interior of La Cle D'or Guesthouse. The Rochambeau Suite features a 1920s cloth-mahogany bedroom suite with French-Rococo style furnishings.

The Spencer-Silver Mansion was built in 1896 on the corner of Bourbon Street at 200 South Union Avenue. Now a bed & breakfast inn, this Port Deposit granite structure is the only high Victorian stone mansion in town.

Par Excellence. Old World Victorian Day Spa, operated by Rosemarie Miller, is located at 450 Congress Avenue. This house was built in 1901.

Currier House Bed & Breakfast at 800 South Market Street. The builder is unknown. Five generations of the Currier family have lived there since 1861.

421 South Union Avenue at Revolution Street was once the Colonial Hotel. The structure now houses medical offices.

The ThoroFair building at 220 North Washington Street.
Built in 1896, the store presently operates as a fine art gallery.

The Turret-towered Maryland House at 200 North Washington Street.

The Seneca Pointe condominiums are a new construction along the Susquehanna Riverfront.

Seneca Warehouse Antiques Mall is located at 201 St. John Street. It was built in 1880 by Stephen J. Seneca to be used as a fruit packing and can manufacturing operation.

810 Giles Street is an example of the many cottage and cape-code styled homes in Havre de Grace built in the twentieth century.

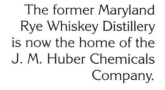

The former Maryland Rye Whiskey Distillery is now the home of the J. M. Huber Chemicals Company.

The James Fahey House was built circa 1898. It's located at 209 North Union Avenue.

Formerly La Maison Des Grecques Greco Art Gallery, this house was built circa 1890 at 215-217 North Union Avenue. It was once a restaurant with rooms upstairs to rent. Today, it's a private residence.

Chapter Three

Around Town

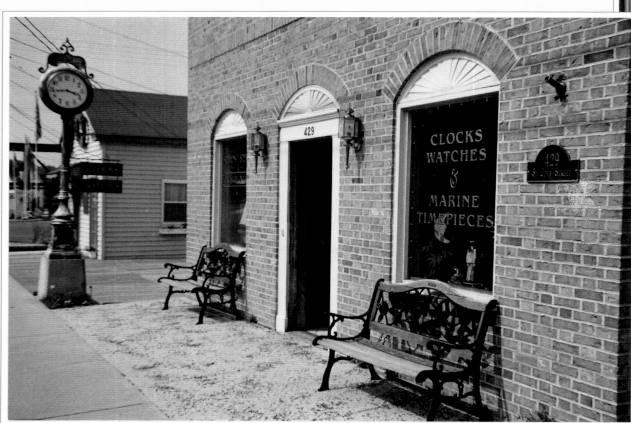

Stephens & Stephens Clock, Watches & Marine Timepieces Shop is located at 429 St. John Street.

Rochambeau Plaza was named for the French general the Count De Rochambeau, whose troops passed through here in 1781 en route to Yorktown, Virginia.

Investment Antiques at 123 Market Street is one of many unusual and delightful business in Havre de Grace featuring an eclectic inventory.

An urn of flowers at 215 North Union Avenue.

Interior of Investment Antiques.

Proprietor John Klisavage is shown in the interior of Washington Street Books.

Mount Erin Cemetery at Angel's Hill in Havre de Grace.

Washington Street Books is located at 131 Washington Street and features an astounding mix of rare and antique books, comics, and other memorabilia.

This Gregorian townhouse built in 1788 at 226 North Washington Street is the most significant historic structure in the city and is commonly known as the Elizabeth Rodgers House. The house was visited by George Washington (documented 1787-1795).

An antique shop on Market Street in Havre de Grace.

A view of the Chesapeake Bay by the lighthouse at the Promenade.

A view of downtown Havre de Grace, looking north on Washington Street from Congress Avenue.

A Victorian cast iron urn sits at 229 North Union Avenue.

The Gazebo on the Promenade by the Chesapeake Bay and Havre de Grace Yacht Basin offers a magnificent view of the Susquehanna flats.

The bronze statute of Major General Marquis de Lafayette at Legion Square and Union Avenue.

Amtrak passing over Havre de Grace on the Pennsylvania Railroad Bridge, erected in 1906, over Otsego and Water streets.

A Maryland Historic Marker notes Old Post Road, which was built in 1666. At Susquehanna Lower Ferry, a former name for Havre de Grace, a public ferry was ordered to be established by the Council of Maryland in 1695 for travel between the north and south. General George Washington and many notable men used this ferry, as did the Continental Army and soldiers of the War between the States (Civil War). The marker was erected by the City of Havre de Grace in celebration of its Bicentennial in 1985.

Chapter Four

Restaurants

The Bayou Restaurant is located on Route 40.

The Chesapeake Hotel Restaurant, now Ken's Steak and Ribs, was once called the Crazy Swede. The hotel and restaurant are old, and are rumored to have hosted Al Capone. The restaurant is located at Franklin Street and North Union Avenue.

The Tidewater Grille rests on the Susquehanna River shore at #300, at the foot of Franklin Street.

MacGregor's Restaurant Tavern and Banquet Room is situated at the foot of Franklin Street on the waterfront.

Price's Seafood was established in 1944 at 654 Water Street. A barn was dismantled from the former Havre de Grace racetrack to build the front part of this restaurant.

Interior of the Chat N Chew Bar area.

Chat N Chew Restaurant and Bar is located at 142 North Washington Street in the lower floor of a brick apartment building.

Java by the Bay Coffee Shop at 118 North Washington Street features special blends and brews.

The Havre de Grace Ritz at 100 North Washington Street is a quaint little restaurant in a Victorian storefront.

Interior of the Havre de Grace Ritz.

An enterprise of the Coakley family, Irish Coakley's Pub is located at 406 St. John Street in a storefront that dates back to 1903.

The *Lantern Queen* is a replica of a nineteenth century steamship
pulling out of dock in Havre de Grace.

Right:
Havre de Grace: Where hospitality awaits you.

Chapter Five

The Marinas and Chesapeake Bay

The Tidewater Marina at the foot of Congress Avenue, 100 Bourbon Street.

Kayaks dot the shoreline of the Susquehanna River.

The Havre de Grace Promenade is a half-mile boardwalk that follows the shoreline and overlooks the confluence of the Susquehanna River and the Chesapeake Bay. Completed in the 1990s, it was extensively damaged by Tropical Storm Isabel in 2003. Through the combined heroic efforts of the city and county governments, the citizens, and volunteers, the Promenade was restored in one year.

A family enjoys fishing by the Chesapeake Bay.

Canadian geese in the Chesapeake Bay.

Two friends are fishing by the Chesapeake Bay from the fishing pier at Frank J. Hutchins Memorial Park, named for a former mayor of Havre de Grace.

View of the Chesapeake Bay: At one time, eight hundred miles of upper watershed flowed uninterrupted here into the Susquehanna River and Chesapeake Bay before the Conowingo Dam and the power plant were built upriver in 1929.

HAVRE DE GRACE

WAR OF 1812

HERE ON THE MORNING OF MAY 3, 1813, BRITISH FORCES UNDER ADMIRAL COCKBURN LANDED, SACKED, AND BURNED THE TOWN. THE PRINCIPAL DEFENSES WERE TWO SMALL BATTERIES ON CONCORD POINT. THE "POTATO BATTERY" ON HIGH GROUND, WAS MANNED TO THE LAST BY JOHN O'NEILL.

MARYLAND HISTORICAL SOCIETY

View of the Chesapeake Bay: Mallard ducks preen themselves on the tidal flats of the Havre de Grace waterfront.

Concord Point Lighthouse Park at Lafayette Street.

View of the Chesapeake Bay: Seagulls wade the Susquehanna River Flats.

THIS MARKER SIGNIFIES THE POINT WHERE THE BEAUTIFUL
SUSQUEHANNA RIVER COMPLETES ITS 444 MILE JOURNEY
TO MEET THE CHESAPEAKE BAY

Presented to
CITY OF HAVRE DE GRACE

by the
SUSQUEHANNA RIVER BASIN COMMISSION
MAY 18, 1995

Fishing by the Chesapeake Bay. By 1760, salted herring
from the Susquehanna Flats at Havre de Grace were
sold in most of the thirteen colonies.

Twenty-seven steps of
Port Deposit granite takes
one to the top of the
lighthouse, thirty-two feet
high. The lighthouse was
completed on May 21,
1827 by Havre de Grace
native John Donahoo.
It was decommissioned
in 1975 and restored in
1979. The Lighthouse
was automated in 1928.
A wedding by the
Concord Point
Lighthouse.

Right:
The Lantern Queen Riverboat on the Susquehanna River Flats.

Sailing the Susquehanna River Flats with the Pennsylvania Railroad Bridge and the Thomas J. Hatem Bridge shown in the background. Also shown are Garrett Island and the City of Perryville.

Chapter Six

Houses of Prayer

The Havre de Grace United Methodist Church at 101 South Union Avenue, with its Gothic-styling, is undoubtedly the most imposing structure in town. The congregation has existed since 1821. This new building was built in 1901 with a gift of money from local cannery businessman, Stephen J. Seneca. As a condition of this gift, the congregation furnished the interior of the church with pews made of white oak, while the altar, pulpit, and choir loft are composed of San Domingo mahogany. The building material is random ashlar granite, quarried nearby at Port Deposit, Maryland. The trim is of Indiana limestone. Over the years, the copper trimming has acquired a rich, green patina.

Window of the Havre de Grace United Methodist Church.

Left:
The grand organ at Havre de Grace United Methodist Church.
The Reverend Edward E. Heydt is presently the pastor.

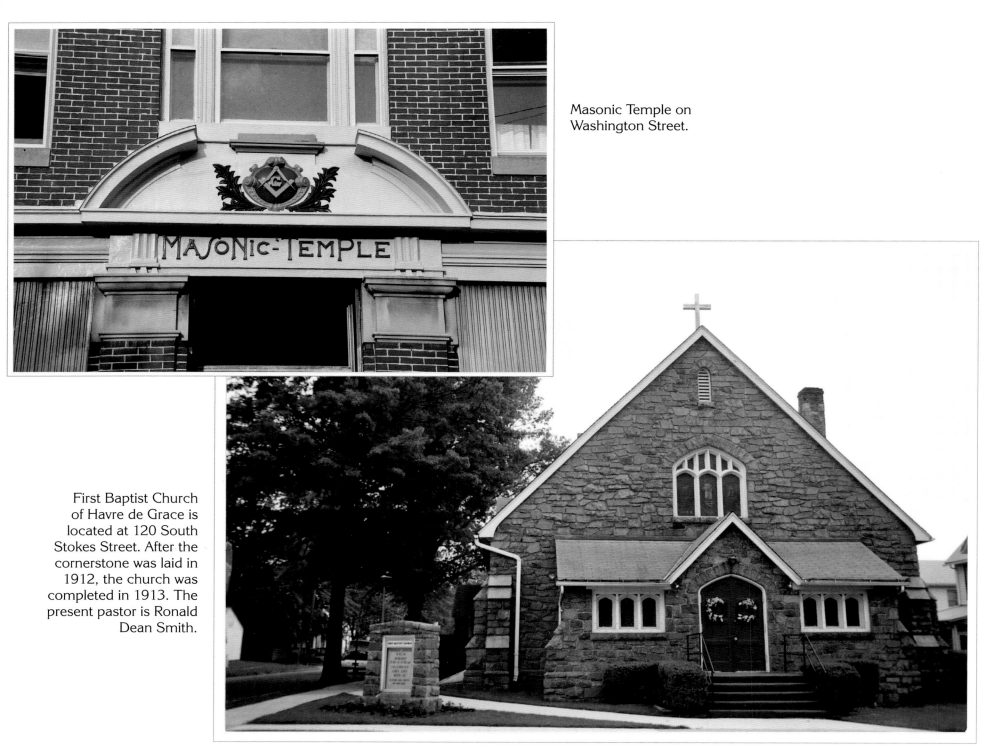

Masonic Temple on Washington Street.

First Baptist Church of Havre de Grace is located at 120 South Stokes Street. After the cornerstone was laid in 1912, the church was completed in 1913. The present pastor is Ronald Dean Smith.

Temple Adas Shalom and Harford Jewish Center nestles along Route 155.

The stained glass transom over the entrance of St. Matthews AUMP Church.

The first and oldest church…
St. John's Church at the corner
of Congress and 121 North
Union avenues. The land
was given to the church by
William Stokes. Earlier he had
envisioned it as a site of the
U.S. Capitol Building. Havre
de Grace was once considered
for the site of the National
Capital city, but missed the
great honor by one vote in
the Senate. Completion of
the church building was twice
delayed; first by a windstorm
and then by the British attack
upon Havre de Grace in 1813.
The church was completed
by 1831. The Reverend John
Elledge is presently the rector.

Sunday morning at St. John's Episcopal Church. Havre de Grace's oldest house of worship is still standing.

St. Matthew African Union Methodist Protestant Church. Located at 563 Revolution Street, the church was built circa 1880. At first, the church was known as Manley's Chapel, but on June 28, 1927, it was renamed St. Matthew AUMP Church. The Reverend Deborah Collins is presently the pastor.

St. James African Methodist Episcopal Church is the oldest black church in Havre de Grace. It's located at 617 Green Street. From 1864-1868 the church was known by the name Ebenezer. On September 2, 1868, it was renamed St. James African Methodist Episcopal Church. The Rev. Franklin J. West has been the pastor there since 1989.

Dating back to 1907, St. Patrick's Catholic Church is located at the corner of Congress Avenue and Stokes Street. The pastor is William J. O'Brien, III.

Chapter Seven

Museums

The Havre de Grace Decoy Museum. The museum occupies the re-conditioned and re-modeled power plant of the old Bayou Hotel.

Wax life-like figures of the old decoy carving masters such as R. Madison Mitchell embellish the museum's exhibits.

The exhibits explain the craft of sailing and hunting through the history of the upper Chesapeake Bay region. This mural and walkway serve as examples.

The museum contains beautiful exhibits of wildfowl decoys like this wooden duck decoy.

The Concord Point Lighthouse at Concord and Lafayette streets in Havre de Grace was built in 1827. It is one of eight lighthouses in the northern bay area built by Havre de Grace native John Donahoo. The first keeper of the lighthouse was John O'Neill, a hero of the War of 1812.

Built in 1840, the Lock House served the lock tender and toll keeper of the first lock of the Susquehanna and Tidewater Canal. This was the first of twenty-nine locks made of Port Deposit granite serving the forty-five-mile canal from Wrightsville, Pennsylvania to Havre de Grace. Locks were usually 150 feet long and eighteen feet wide. The structure housed the lock keeper's family and the canal's business offices. The canal ceased operation in Harford County by 1900.

The Havre de Grace Maritime Museum and boat building school at 100 Lafayette Street. Near the lighthouse is a modern raised structure. The museum is committed to preserving Havre de Grace's vast maritime history.

Left, above, and right:
J. Edmund Bull, who founded the Steppingstone Museum in 1970, stated, "The Steppingstone Museum provides a necessary look into the past." The stone farmhouse dates back to 1771. The museum, located in Susquehanna State Park, is nested on a picturesque hillside overlooking the beautiful Susquehanna River. The house is surrounded by barns and other farm buildings that make an ideal setting for the exhibits and displays for a museum representing rural America from 1880 to 1920. The Steppingstone Museum is a private, non-profit museum located at 461 Quaker Bottom Road.

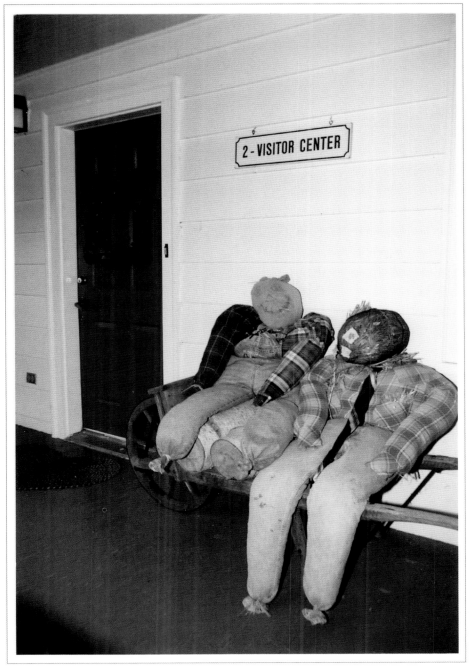

Spinning and weaving loom at the Steppingstone Museum.

The kitchen at the Steppingstone Museum in the stone farmhouse is set up as a late nineteenth century-early twentieth century country home.

The interior of the Steppingstone Museum stone farmhouse. Shown is an office desk with ledger and oil lamp where the farm overseer may have kept his books and records.

The Steppingstone Museum also contains an exhibit of tooth extractors for dog's teeth.

The Foard Blacksmith Shop at the Steppingstone Museum contains twin working forges for metal crafting and ironwork.

Chapter Eight

Susquehanna State Park

A tributary of the Susquehanna River in Susquehanna State Park.

The Rock Run Mill is now part of Susquehanna State Park. It was built in 1794 by Nathaniel Giles and John Stump, prominent businessmen, on land originally known as the "Land of Promise." The mill was in continuous operation until 1954. It is one of the oldest mills standing in Harford County. It still retains its twelve-ton Fitz waterwheel installed in 1900. The wheel is thirty-two feet in diameter and 2½ feet wide with eighty-four buckets.

This stone home, known as the Archer mansion, was constructed in 1804 by John Carter in the town of Rock Run.

Entering the Susquehanna State Park. About three miles north of Havre de Grace off of Route 155, the Maryland state park encompasses 2,200 acres on the west bank of the Susquehanna River.

By the Susquehanna River, at the Susquehanna State Park. The park is the site of nature trails, a bird sanctuary, picnic and camp sites, bicycle paths, and one of the finest fishing grounds on the East Coast.

Waterfalls at Susquehanna State Park. The focal point of Susquehanna State Park is the area called "Land of Promise," the historic area near Rock Run/Lapidum.

Chapter Nine

Swan Harbor

Above, left, and right:
Swan Harbor Farm: Situated on 516 acres, Swan Harbor Farm, a stately home on the Chesapeake Bay, boasts a long and proud history. Initially, the home was owned by several generations of the Giles family in the 1770s, but the most significant owner was John Adlum purchased the farm from Thomas Giles in 1797. Adlum was a banker from Philadelphia.

From Swan Harbor Farm, John Ablum pioneered winemaking in Maryland. In 1809, Mr. Ablum sent a bottle of his fine burgundy to his friend, Thomas Jefferson. Harford County purchased the Swan Harbor Farm in 1994 as part of its open space preservation program.

View of the Chesapeake Bay from Swan Harbor Farm. In the 1830s, early nineteenth century entrepreneur Jacob Hoke of Have de Grace acquired a farm that was then called "Howell's Dream," along with many other Harford County properties.

Chapter Ten

4th of July Celebration

The 4th of July Parade on North Union Avenue is the largest public event in Havre de Grace.

Shown are Maryland National Guard troops in Revolutionary War/Continental Army uniforms.

Many organizations and schools from the entire Harford County, and as far away as Baltimore, are participating in the parade.

An annual patriotic event, the 4th of July Fireworks at Millard E. Tydings Memorial Park over the Susquehanna River Flats.

Right:
The Bulle Rock Golf Course is located at 320 Blenheim Lane in Havre de Grace. This is a national ranked world-class golf course. This Peter Dye designed layout, formerly a horse farm, was Golf Digest's "Best New Upscale Golf Course in America for 1998."

DIRECTIONS: I-95 south into Maryland, exit 89 (Havre de Grace). At the top of the ramp, turn left and follow signs for Route 155 East. Follow Route 155 East for 2.2 miles, bearing right at signs for Route 155 and Route 40. At the light, turn right onto Route 40 West. Follow Route 40 for 1.9 miles. The entrance to Bulle Rock is on the right.

Bulle Rock Golf Course

Public Buildings

Havre de Grace Senior High School on Congress Avenue. This view shows the auditorium and gymnasium, which was built on the site of the first Havre de Grace High School that opened in 1897. A new school was built in 1924.

The Harford County Public Library. The Havre de Grace branch is located at
North Union and Pennington avenues.

Citizens Care and Rehabilitation Center at 414 South Market Street in Havre de Grace.

United States Post Office in Havre de Grace at Juniata and Green streets.

The new Havre de Grace City Hall, built in 1992, was designed by architect Poldi Hirsch who employed fieldstone and elements reminiscent of a lighthouse tower. This is where the City Council meets. City Hall and the new police station are located at 711 Pennington Avenue.

Harford Memorial Hospital at 501 South Union Avenue and Revolution Street is a member of the Upper Chesapeake Health System.

The Fire Department, firehouse #2, at the corner of Pennington and North Union avenues.

The main clubhouse building built in 1922 at the former Havre de Grace Race Track, nicknamed "The Graw." The Harford Agricultural and Breeders Association Racetrack was one of four one-mile thoroughbred racetracks in Maryland and reflected Harford County's status as a breeding center for thoroughbred horses.

Ode to Havre de Grace

O Susquehanna,
hurry down the mountains
and empty your soul
into the Chesapeake Bay.
Havre de Grace
lies there waiting
to wash her tired feet.

As she's gazing across the waters,
she reflects glories of yesterdays:
before the British,
before the fire,
before the eerie moments of the war.
The Presidential inaugural parade
on Congress Avenue was not to be.

O Susquehanna,
hurry down the mountains
and bathe Havre de Grace
into the glorious days of yesterday,
as she struggles to regain her crown
and her rightful place
by the Chesapeake Bay.

Leon Nicholas Kalas
May 29, 1999

Directions

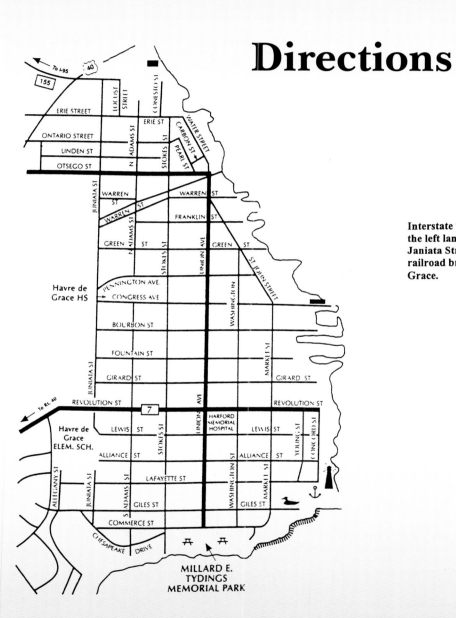

Interstate 95, exit 89 (Havre de Grace), follow Route 155 East for 2.2 miles. Stay in the left lane. Proceed straight under railroad bridge to the end. Make right onto Janiata Street. Follow to 1st light and make left on Otsego Street, bear right under railroad bridge onto North Union Avenue. You are now in Down Town Havre de Grace.